Bison Management Strategies

By

Bob Mahoney

Foreword

As I set out upon this journey and labor of love, I have a feeling of trepidation as well as a slight feeling of fear. This idea of how to manage bison has been gathering itself in my gray matter, first as an inkling or twinge, and then as thoughts began to form, the process started to take on a life of its own.

Bison came into my life when I was a young whippersnapper of four years, and they have been a part of my life ever since. I didn't really become consumed by bison until I read David Diary's *The Buffalo Book*. I became obsessed. I have a grand total of thirty-seven years of hands-on experience dealing with these North American icons, as either a ranch hand or manager at various ranches across the United States. I attended North Dakota State University for eight years without getting my degree, due to lack of funds.

In this book, I will be looking into management strategies, examining what has worked and what hasn't. I will also be relaying incidents along my learning curve—lessons learned, some the hard way. I trust that you will learn that dealing with any animal—not just bison—requires a different mindset than Farragut's "Damn the torpedoes, full speed ahead!" concept that is commonly used.

My hope as you read through the following pages is that you will gain some insight into bison demeanor, society and their lives. Enjoy!

Acknowledgements

I would be remiss if I didn't thank various friends that helped in the process, with reviews and comments.

First, Mark Roundstone, Director of the Northern Cheyenne Nations Natural Resources Department, whose comments at a meeting we both attended planted the seed in my brain for this book.

Arnold Dood , MT Fish, Wildlife and Parks bison program, for his insight and valued comments and helpful hints that I utilized in various sections of this book ; and the various bison producers and friends who gave me jobs, which in turn allowed me to observe their herds. From this I learned what works and what doesn't when working with and around bison. I'm still learning daily.

I would also like to thank Suzzanne Kelly at New Rivers Press for her valuable insight and comments on how to make this manuscript more entertaining and readable.

I would like to thank the bison for their tolerance and teachings, and for allowing me to have a unique perspective into their society.

Last, to my partner in life, Esther Hockett, who periodically read this manuscript and commented on whether I was going astray in my ramblings. I love you, my sweet. Thank you.

Chapter Headings

1) Soil Health

2) Grasses: Nature's Sun Collectors

3) What's for Lunch? A Smorgasbord of Grazing Systems

4) Fencing: A Neighborly Necessity

   1. Commonly Used Types of Fencing

   2. Brace Posts, Creek and River Crossings, Low Spots, and Coulee Crossings

5) Corrals: You Gotta Know When to Hold'em

6) Squeeze Chutes: Like The Walls Closing In:

7) Low-Stress Animal Handling: It Works

8) Corral Designs

9) Bison: Where it All Began

   1. Todays Bison

   2. Migration: Did It Happen?

   3. Behaviors: The Good, The Bad, and The Ugly: Know When To Walk Away, Know When to Run

   4. Personal Encounters

   5. Words of Wisdom

10) Genetics

11) Classification

1) Soil Health

This is probably the most overlooked aspect in the field of grazing and ranch management. I make this statement from having seen the repercussions of both season long grazing and different methods of rotational grazing systems. I don't claim to be an expert on any of these systems, which I will address in the next chapter. Clearly, all of us who make a living from grazing mammals, whether they be cattle, bison, sheep, or any other grazer, are all grass farmers first and stockmen second. Without a healthy soil base, we wouldn't be in the livestock business for very long.

Throughout the written history of our planet, there are accounts of the destruction of healthy soils either through overusing the soil without replenishing vital nutrients or simply by using and abusing the soils until nothing would grow and then moving on. This basically leaves a desert, which may recover over time—but most likely not. Let's take a look at a few of the ingredients necessary and vital for a healthy, productive soil.

Soil health includes an active microbial community. By this, I mean soils filled with millions upon millions of microbes which are continuously breaking down organic matter, which, in turn, provides nutrients and minerals to the plants that feed our animals, who then feed us, and the cycle continues.

A viable healthy soil is one that is able to capture and retain any and all water that falls upon it. There are two demonstrations of this that really made an impact on me, one from college and one from a picture I saw at a holistic management workshop that I attended. The first took place in a basic soils class. Each group in the class had a long plastic tube filled with different soils from around the state, to a depth of roughly three meters. First we moistened the soils slightly at each discernible horizon line in order to gauge how much water was required to pack/roll the soil into a small ball. This gave us an indication as to the porosity (water-gathering capacity) and structure of the soil. If and when we succeeded in making a ball, we were told to stretch the soils as thin as we could. Those with more loamy soils did well, while those with the more sandy soils did not fare as well. This demonstration allowed us to feel the different textures of the soil. This also made me realize that soil is more than just dirt. Soils that have even a slight amount of clay in them will retain more water than plain, sandy soils. Another fact that I became acutely aware of, was at a holistic Management work shop that I attended. This was a picture that showed the amount of damage that a drop of rain does to bare ground. If the force of one raindrop is enough to scatter small soil particles everywhere, one can only imagine the results of a severe thunderstorm. Trickles lead to runoff, which leads to erosion and washing away of valuable topsoil. We need to keep that bare ground covered.

The final sign of a healthy, viable soil is a mineral cycle, or the ongoing breakdown of both rocks and organic matter from which the soils receive vital nutrients and minerals. This is accomplished by pressure, water, soil microbes, and time. It doesn't take very long to lose a healthy soil base (i.e. leaving ground bare, not using natural fertilizer, no legumes, and most importantly, allowing a significant rest period between periods of use). However, it takes thousands of years to replace one inch of lost topsoil. My hope is that these important concepts will ring a bell and allow ranchers and farmers to realize that without a healthy soil base, we cannot feed the world; we will expend one of the most vital natural productive resources we have—our soils.

I once worked at a bison ranch in central Pennsylvania. I was charged with fencing a forty-acre patch and getting grass to grow among the rocks and debris to supplement the other two pastures. This was the top of the hill pasture. We all know that it is risky to try to develop a pasture in those conditions, but we were successful up to a point. The grass grew, and I let the herd into this upper pasture for a couple of days. When I moved all 120 head down below, the other two pastures hadn't had sufficient time for regrowth. It became a never-ending struggle for animal survival, with me wanting to feed hay and boss telling me no. I had made a habit of mowing and dragging each pasture and closing the gates to let the pasture rest and recoup, but to no avail. The next day when I would come in to work, the gate was open and the bison were in the pastures. The point of all this is to show you that there were several dynamics involved in this operation. The pastures were overused to the point of ruining the health of this property. We were overstocked, and we should have left the main herd up on the mountain twelve miles away. We were trying to run an exuberant number of animals on a small amount of acreage.

The boss wouldn't listen to reason; it didn't fit with his management plan or style. He claimed that he needed over one hundred head of animals to make it a profitable business venture, yet at what cost? He lost Me., this was before I had decided to go to school and learn a little about soil and range management. I had used pasture rotation at a previous place of employment; it worked well; more on this in the next chapter.

I'll use this as a segue into the next chapter about grasses, nature's sun collectors.

2) Grasses: **Nature's Sun Collectors**

Which grasses are best for raising animals? This has been a much-debated subject. Where I reside, if there is abundant sunshine and water and a healthy soil, we can use almost any grass that grows, with the exception of Japanese brome and cheatgrass. We don't want to foster the growth of large stands of crested wheatgrass either, as it is edible to most grazers only in the early spring. After that it becomes very bitter.

Japanese brome and cheatgrass are both highly invasive species that are only medium to poor fodder at the best of times, and they replace good species of grasses if you allow heavy grazing and give the pastures no rest. When I worked at a bison ranch for a part of the summer, one of my tasks was to mow around a couple of barns by the feedlot. On a relatively slow day, I went to the headquarters, got the riding lawnmower, and started mowing around the barns in one section where there was about an acre and a half of both of these noxious grasses. As I mowed around the outside edges, the grasses became taller and thicker. It took me two hours just to mow this section down, and I itched and coughed for three days afterward. Animals won't even touch these two types of grasses as they mature because the seed heads will stick to their fur or hide, get in their eyes, and burrow into the sides of their mouths and tongues if they eat it in the mature stage. This causes weight loss and ultimately starvation.

In the ideal range system for grazing either native or domestic grazers, there would be a good mix of various grasses (C-3 cool season and C-4 warm seasons), sedges (grass like plants), and a variety of legumes that are natural nitrogen fixers. Legume plants such as clovers, through the nodules on their roots, release nitrogen into the surrounding soil for use by other plants.

C-3 grasses are the grasses that grow and produce during spring and fall, provided they have adequate moisture and a healthy soil base. Some of these C-3 grasses are Kentucky bluegrass, orchard grass, June grass, and smooth brome.

C-4 grasses are typically native grasses that evolved on the prairie; they tend to be productive during the warmest times of the growing season. C-4 grasses are typically drought resistant and make great fodder, high in nutritional value. Some types of C-4 grasses are gamma grass, buffalo grass, switch grass, little and big bluestem, and needle-and-thread grass.

Native grasses, sedges, and legumes evolved on the Great Plains along with the grazers (native ungulates) that utilized them, such as bison, pronghorn antelope, various species of the deer family, and the rodent population (mainly prairie dogs). Also included in this list of native grazers would be the insect population, mainly locusts and grasshoppers. These grasses are usually drought resistant, and they evolved through heavy periods of grazing, after which the native ungulates would move on. This would equate to a high-impact, short-term grazing cycle. The native grazers would be good for the soils of the area with their hoof action and the deposition of their dung and urine. Their movements across the prairies would leave litter as ground cover, along with patches of grasses and sedges on the areas they currently grazed. The animals' hooves would break up the soil cap that allowed water and their natural fertilizer, along with colonies of dung beetles, to fertilize the soils. After these herds of native grazers moved to a new area searching for food, they might not return to the prior area for a year or more, which resulted in rest and recovery of the grazing area.

In any large grazing plan, used by large grazers, bison, for example—the animals would be found spread out over the area in small *family groups*. These groups are made up of ten to twenty individuals, mainly cows and their calves, young stock, yearlings, and two-year-olds. Mature bison bulls and adolescent bulls also stay together in smaller groups away from the main herd until breeding season draws near.

3) What's for Lunch? A Smorgasbord of Grazing Systems

- Open range
- Season long
- Pasture rotation
- Low density/low frequency
- High density/high frequency
- Mob grazing
- Holistic management

I will give you a description of what each of these systems of grazing entails, and then you can investigate further and decide for yourself which is best for your operation.

Open-range grazing took place in the late 1800s on much of the Great Plains. This style of grazing closely mimicked how the native grazers utilized the landscape. Groups of cattlemen would move their herds of cattle around to fresh grass on new pastures every couple of days so their cattle could eat the new grass and get fat for market in the fall. This system lasted until the invention of barbwire in 1874. The big ranches of the West were either sold off or broken up, or they stayed the same except they were fenced in.

Season long grazing is probably the system used for the longest period of time. It was employed following the days of open-range grazing, and it is exactly what the term states. The farmer or rancher would put all of the cattle or sheep or whatever grazers they had on the same pasture to stay there for the whole season until they rounded them up in the fall. Season-long grazing had many flaws, such as overgrazing within the pasture, increasing bare ground, and noxious weeds and invasive grass species replacing native grasses, to name a few.

Cattle and sheep are not the native grazers that evolved on the Great Plains. They tend to graze more or less in one spot and not utilize the whole pasture unless they are forced to move to a different area within the pasture. These favorite grazing spots are usually within a mile of a water source.

Bison tend to graze their whole pasture daily unless they are restricted in their movement. They don't graze in the same spot because they are always on the move. They rotationally graze on their own. Bison will graze two or more miles from a source of water.

Pasture rotation is one of the newer grazing systems that have been brought forth over the last forty to fifty years. The following systems have come forth in an effort to more closely mimic how native grazers utilized their range. With a limited amount of land available to grazers across this country, it behooves the rancher or farmer to make the best use of the lands that are available. Hence, we tend to break large pastures into smaller pastures with cross fencing, thus creating more pastures for our animals to use.

There are a few things we must be aware of when utilizing any of the following systems. These systems are all dependent on the number of animals and the duration, or time they stay in each pasture. Both are dependent on the amount of forage available. Also, monitor the grass within each pasture daily so you will know if you need to move the animals sooner than planned.

I will use the example of a bison ranch I helped set up in Pennsylvania. This ranch was roughly 110 acres in size. We divided it into eighteen pastures/paddocks ranging in size from three acres to eighteen acres. Each group of bison had three pastures, which we rotated the group through. Groups consisted of ten cows, their calves, and a bull, so we had the potential for a herd size of twenty-one bison per group. The exception was one group that consisted of two "pet" older cows, an injured bull, and three yearling bulls. We rotated this group among the four smaller pastures. We generally didn't move the groups to new pastures until they had been grazing anywhere from twenty-five to thirty days on the old pastures. I monitored the grass throughout each pasture, and when it was getting close to four inches high, I would move each group to its next pasture in the rotation. Each paddock was mowed and harrowed using a flex-tooth drag/harrow to break up manure clods and break up the soil cap. I allowed these pastures to rest for roughly sixty days before its group returned. Grass was always abundant, of course; Pennsylvania has a more humid, rainy type of climate than the Great Plains, which is a dryer, more brittle environment.

Low density/low frequency and high density/high frequency grazing are systems with a lower or higher number of animals in a paddock for a longer or shorter time frame. Smaller numbers of animals are able to stay in a paddock longer without deleterious effects on the paddock. The length of time is dependent on grass height. For higher numbers of animals on the same pasture, the stay will be shorter—usually no more than two to three days, depending on the number of animals in the group. Again, the length of time is dependent of the height of the grass.

With mob grazing, you would keep very high numbers of animals in a pasture for very short periods of time, usually hours. This entails using mobile electric pasture wires and grazing one-, two-, or three-acre pastures for the ultimate positive effect on the land, along with a resting regrowth period before allowing the animals to utilize the paddock again.

You must learn to be flexible when using any of the above systems, as regrowth of the grasses in each of the multiple paddocks may be slower than you expected. Should that happen, you may need to move the animals to a different paddock than the one you were originally planning to move your animals to.

Holistic Management is a concept brought forth by Alan Savory in the 1980s for the improvement of land management through the use of grazing animals. This is a life-defining way of utilizing various management tools, including testing questions, a feedback loop, to guide you in your decision-making process by encompassing all aspects or *wholes* as a more effective management tool. You start the process by listing a few thoughts with all stakeholders in the operation of the ranch, farm, your personal life, etc. From everyone's input regarding what they want for the operation and themselves, you join together to form a holistic goal for the operation, which you revisit yearly to see how close you are to reaching this goal. A visit to the Holistic Management webpage (http://holisticmanagement.org/) and attending various workshops around the country will leave you wanting more information on this innovative way of making a healthy environment through the use of grazers.

Alan Savory and Jody Butterfield's book, *Holistic Management: A New Framework for Decision Making* is a must-read for anyone who is interested in range, ranch, pasture, and farm management.

I will list the seven test questions in no specific order except for the last question, which Mister Savory states is the question you need to ask if your idea passes all of the other questions. Here are the questions: Cause and Effect: Does the decision address the root cause of the problem?

Marginal reaction: Will this idea provide the greatest return toward the company's holistic goal for the time and monies spent?

Weakest link: Toward the social, biological, or financial, can your proposal pass all of the questions involved in finding your operation's weakest link in terms of your holistic goal?

Sustainability: Will your decision/action lead you toward or away from your holistic goal?

Energy/money source and use: Is the energy/money derived from the best or most appropriate source?

Gross profit analysis: Which parts of this operation contribute most to covering the overhead of my operation?'

Society and culture: This is a three-part question, and it asks how you feel about your action? Will it lead you toward the quality of life you desire? Will your action adversely affect the lives of other people within your operation? Once you start using these test questions to make decisions concerning your operations management, you will find yourself using them for almost any decisions you make concerning your operation and your life.

4) Fencing: A Neighborly Necessity

In today's technology-driven world, we seem to be obsessed, to the point of overkill, with regard to bison fencing. When you look back into history, you find that Paleolithic man used whatever was handy to contain large ungulates in the process of obtaining food.

In my thirty-six-plus years of bison management, I have observed and built numerous bison fences. These fences ranged from a simple four-wire barbwire fence to an eight-foot net wire fence. A lot of these earlier fences were either four-foot net wire with one or two strands of barbwire six to eight inches apart above the net wire or straight barbwire with five to six strands. They did the job well. Granted, if the bison felt the need to go somewhere else, they could without any problem. Bison will stay in any pasture you want them in as long as they have plenty of grass, adequate water and minerals, and enough room to escape from a more dominant bison. If bison are confined in too small an area without adequate room for escape, they are bound to go through fences just to escape a more dominant bison. This leads me to state a fact: man hasn't built a fence yet that will contain bison if they want out.

Fencing has an impact on other wildlife, most notably the pronghorn antelope. Pronghorns, for all their speed and agility, tend not to jump fences. They will plow into them and become entangled, and either die from stress overload trying to escape or starve to death. This is not a pretty picture. There have been documented cases of antelope jumping fences, but they would rather go under them. If the bottom wire is less than fourteen inches, antelope will attempt to go under them and become caught. That is why I, along with other conservation entities, recommend that the bottom wire of the fence be at least fourteen inches above ground level.

I was privileged a couple of weeks ago to visit with Robbie Magnum, director of the Fort Peck Fish, Wildlife and Parks Division. He took three bison advocates on a tour of the Yellowstone and Reservations Bison project. We viewed the infamous "Yellowstone 61" shortly after their arrival at Fort Peck. We went on a tour of their new pasture, which was fenced with a six-strand combination barbed and twisted smooth wire wildlife-friendly fence. The bottom and top wires were smooth. The bottom wire was sixteen inches off the ground, with the next four barbwires spaced ten inches apart. The top smooth wire was ten inches above the fourth barbwire; this allowed antelope to go under the bottom wire unrestricted and deer to easily jump over the top. Robbie is in the process of putting the finishing touches on this project by stringing one electric wire in the center of the perimeter fence three inches off the fence posts as a deterrent to the bison coming close to the fences.

4.1) Commonly Used Types of Wire

Barbwire, usually fourteen gauge, has two or four barbs evenly placed along the length of the wire. This wire is full of stretch and spring. It is fairly hard to work with. You must use care when stringing this wire so that you don't inadvertently become caught up in it.

Rolled net wire is somewhat flexible and can be purchased in varying heights from twenty-four inches up to seven feet. This type of fencing is manufactured like a net, either with small openings at the bottom and the largest opening on the top, or the same size openings all the way through. You can buy stretchers built specifically for net wire. Most producers who use this type of fencing make their own, using two 2x6s a little longer than the wire and bolts to fasten the boards together. A chain attached to both top and bottom allows you to stretch all points of the wire evenly.

High-tensile/smooth wire fence is probably the most economical type of fencing to construct per mile. It can be purchased and built relatively easily once you have all the posts in the ground. This wire goes up quickly. You can add electricity to any of the wires by placing rubber tube insulators on the hot wires. Also, it behooves you to keep plant growth from covering up the hot wires; it will always stay charged. There is one big drawback to using this type of wire: It is very unforgiving. Once you've ratcheted the wire tight, if an animal gets a foot wrapped up in the wire, it is like a death trap. If you don't find the animal and cut the wire, the animal will slowly starve to death or die from the stress of being entangled in the wire. The more the animal struggles to get loose, the tighter the wire gets. Even if you release it from the wire, the damage has most likely been done. The animal will probably lose its hoof or foot eventually.

High-tensile barbwire is a relatively new type of barbwire. It doesn't have the spring that regular barbwire has; yet it is really easy to work with. After you learn the trick for splicing the wire together, you can find yourself building a lot of fence very easily. Once the wire is tightened, it stays tight. I haven't heard of any detrimental effects from any of the bison ranches where this wire has been used.

4.2) Brace Posts—Stream and River Crossings—Coulee and Low-Spot Fencing

Brace posts are a necessary, useful part of any fence. If you are fencing a long, relatively flat stretch, one set of brace posts every half mile works well. You would use this H-type arrangement as a point to tighten and fasten your wires to. These brace posts can be constructed of either steel (two-inch well stem pipe), wood, or a combination of the two. I have seen and used all three. An essential part of the wood and wood-pipe combination is the brace wires. These are just smooth wires wrapped around both top and bottom of the brace posts and then tightened, usually with a chunk of wood to help secure and strengthen the brace posts to keep them from being pulled out of the ground, a good rule to remember when running brace wires is "top of the run to bottom of the line."

Creek and river crossings can be quite a challenge to fence, especially if they are prone to times of high water. Whatever you use, it needs to be flexible, and after periods of high water, you need to clean the debris off the wire, as it adds a lot of extra weight and loosens the wire. With river and creek crossings, you need to be aware of the depth of the cut (i.e., the top of the bank to the riverbed), steepness of the bank, and the width of the crossing. Also, you need to be aware of the type of soil you are attempting to build your fence on. If it is a gumbo-type soil, your brace posts will need to be a sufficient distance from the flood plain to be able to support the fence during high water.

Low spots, hills, coulees, or anywhere that snow drifts across are almost always a challenge for keeping the fence in place and your animals in. I have viewed and helped construct some fences in parts of this country where ingenuity has helped save the day as far as keeping animals contained during blizzards or other periods of foul weather. Whenever possible, fence around these trouble spots. If you need to follow the contour of the land, use materials such as well stem and sucker rod to cross these areas. In general, I would build fences in these areas the way I would construct a corral fence, only at the height of the fence run where you place it. These fences would include upright posts two to three feet taller than your fence, a top rail welded and connected to the uprights, and a sucker rod welded and clipped horizontally to uprights every ten inches except at the bottom, which would be fourteen to sixteen inches off the ground. This will allow antelope to cross under. I will explore this topic further in the next chapter on corrals.

In the case of an area of the pasture, such as a large coulee or arroyo, where snow tends to drift and accumulate, I would build a corral-type fence for bison, seven feet minimum height. I would more than likely build this fence on the high pasture side, in effect fencing out the coulee.

5) **Corrals: You Got to Know When to Hold 'Em!**

If you are raising bison, or planning on raising bison, at some point you will need a corral system. Whether you are raising them for profit, conservation, or just to have them around, you need some way to gather them up and contain them for doctoring, culling, or loading for transport. These corral systems must be big enough to handle all animals in the herd, with safety being a priority for both the animals and the workers.

There are three main styles of corral systems. These are: an open system, a closed system, and a semi-closed system. I have worked bison through all three systems. I prefer the open or the semi-closed. When I started in the bison business, it was a relatively new profession. The resources that we have today weren't readily available, so for me, the learning curve was quite high and hard. We generally worked the bison the way cattleman worked cattle. You did it on the ground at their level, whooping and hollering all the way. Looking back on it now, it's a wonder that we didn't lose or injure more animals or people, or have more wrecks than we did. One thing I learned was how to read the animal, which I accomplished through spending hours observing the bison, both in the pasture setting and in the corral. This taught me about their daily lives, their interactions with one another, and their environment. These observations also taught me how to work bison on their level, without creating unnecessary wrecks. I will continue this discussion in the next chapter.

The open type of corral system is usually made with pipe, typically four-inch or two-inch pipe, or two-inch pipe and sucker rod. This system is designed so you can see the animals and they can see you. With this openness, you can also work the bison either within or from the outside of the corral alleyways. This also gives you a way out if necessary.

The semi-closed system is relatively solid on the bottom four feet of the alleyways, with just enough room between the boards for climbing out of the way if need be. This system works well, especially for calves, as opposed to the open system, where they tend to try to climb through the sucker rod and break horns and sometimes other parts.

The closed corral system, to me, is like an accident waiting to happen. This corral has straight, solid-looking walls seven feet tall, and you work the bison from above, from catwalks. I have always found that the bison tend to be more antsy and harder to work when you are attempting to get them to respond to your movements from above. This goes back to the predator-prey animal concept. We are the predator getting ready to pounce from above. Don't get the wrong idea. It can be done easily. However, in general, unless you are aware of what you need to do to initiate movement and get a favorable response, you are wasting your time.

All corrals need a place or group of small narrow pens, not any wider than the back opening of the chute, where you can hold the next one or two animals to go through the chute. These holding pens need three things: First, they need to be semi-open with a top over them, to guard against the bison from trying to exit over the top. Second, they shouldn't be over thirty-four inches wide.

Third, they need a moveable gate on the working side that will be shoved in toward the rear of the bison, especially calves, to keep them headed in the right direction. The stop for these gates would be a timber hung on the gate, which is dropped between the gate and post. I observed this in a handling demonstration at the 777 Bison Ranch in South Dakota. It saves a lot of headaches if a calf gets turned around.

I recently had the opportunity to help work some bison through the Bad River Ranches handling facility. The members of the crew at the ranch usually handle around seven thousand head of bison or more every year and can get the job done within a two-week period, averaging close to five hundred head of bison a day. A lot of thought and planning went into the final design of this corral system. It takes two people on the outside of the working facility bringing the animals up to be processed. The animals are worked quietly; there is no yelling, waving of arms, etc. As they are brought into the building, from the teardrop pen, they go two ways, either to the right or straight ahead. All sorting is done hydraulically. Animals are kept usually three to a box, with four boxes surrounding the operator's station. The operator's station is above the boxes, and it is usually necessary to have one crew member on either side, on the ground, to help move animals up to the pen behind the squeeze chute. This pen has a double door, one of which is solid, that swings over to keep the animals headed in the right direction.

This is one of the quickest, most efficient handling facilities that I have had the privilege to work bison through; it is both open and semi-open. We worked 278 head of bison through it in the space of two and a half hours, not counting the hour-and-a-half repair time on the chute. There is always something happening when you work bison. The system used at Bad River Ranches is a Berlinic handling system, made in Canada.

6) Squeeze Chutes: Like a Wall Closing In

There are several different makes of squeeze chutes available on the market today. However, not too many are manufactured specifically for bison. Whether these chutes are manual or hydraulic, they all need to be big enough to accommodate the largest animal in your herd and not be so tall that the operator of the chute needs to be a giant. There are two requirements for the chute to be considered bison tough: solid bars across the top of the chute and a crash gate. This crash gate is vital in order to capture and stop the bison, as they move faster than you can close the head gate.

There are different makers of chutes. These manufactures produce either V-bottom or straight-sided chutes.

The V-bottom chute is made according to the contour of the large ungulate. It is adjustable, meaning that the side on the bottom will slide in or out to accommodate the size of the bison. Powder River makes an excellent V- bottom bison chute that doesn't use ropes anywhere. There can be a couple of big problems with ropes dangling from chutes, these are: 1) the operator has the potential to get hung up in the ropes, 2) there is always the possibility of grabbing the wrong rope and turning the animal loose when a member of the crew is standing in harm's way.

The straight-sided chute has sides that come in or squeeze the animals to keep them relatively still. It is always a good idea to leave the width of your fist between the side of the animal and the side of the chute. A good example of a straight-sided manual chute is a Pearson chute. Squeeze chutes are likened to a room where the walls are closing in around you. How would that make you feel?

Various companies manufacture hydraulic chutes, including both of the aforementioned companies. From reports that I've heard from various bison producers, the Pearsall chute is the newest and best hydraulic chute on the market. I can't say either way. I've never seen or used one. The Silencer chute is the one everyone with large herds considered to be the top of the line. That brings a point to mind. A producer needs to have some idea as to how large his or her operation is going to be, how many animals they are running, in order to determine the cost of the squeeze chute. If your operation is smaller than 150 head of bison, the cost of a manual squeeze chute can be justified; the same goes for the hydraulic chute—anything over 150 or two hundred head is an economic feasibility.

7) Low-Stress Animal Handling: It Works

When working your bison or setting up the design of the corral system, it is necessary that you are aware of how a bison's behaviors come into play. In the corral, bison will always try to move in the direction from which they came. You need to design the corral system with that in mind and use it to your advantage. If you design a system for your herd size, make it look as if they are heading back out the gate they came in through. However, instead of going out, they head down through the working alleys. Work small groups or half the herd as long as there is sufficient room to accommodate all sizes of animals. Herd bulls should be sorted off and be back out in the pasture when you're working cows and calves.

Low-stress handling deals with using the natural behaviors of the bison to your advantage (i.e., going back the way they came). If they are turned around in a wider alley, just lightly poke them in the flank with a sorting stick or your fingers, and they will turn around. Don't wave small flags in their face, as this will just upset them and make them harder to work. There are only two times when a Hot-Shot tool is needed when working bison. First, if you are pregnancy checking cows and if the cow sits down in the chute, just place the end of the Hot-Shot between her toes and zap her once. She will immediately stand. Second, if a bison stalls out and won't move, zap him or her only once under the tail. These are the only times I will ever use a Hot-Shot on bison.

Some producers have a hard time getting bison into a squeeze chute. This is a relatively simple task, especially if the bison can see you. A step or two toward them at a brisk pace (against the grain), into or past their shoulder area, will move them forward. This tactic also works well when you're working bison at ground level outside the alley fence, though you might need to take a step toward their shoulder to get them to move forward. If you want them to stop, turn around and walk the other way (with the grain).

Low-stress handling techniques were reborn back in the nineteen eighties and nineties by several people. I first read about them in *The Stockmen Grass Farmer* magazine. The article was about Bud Williams, a rancher who read about how the Spaniards had handled large herds of sheep and cattle easily. He tried some of their techniques, polished them up, and taught us some of the animal's behaviors, which benefitted both the animals and handlers.

You will find all my references and additional resources at the end of this book. One last thought: I have found that it is easier to start working bison in the morning hours, from 7:00 to 8:30 a.m., as the bison, to me, seem to be a little slow and not as sharp as they are later in the day.

To practice these techniques, watching your animals is always a good place to start. When I first started using these techniques, I would pick a spot several hundred yards away and start walking toward it. I would attempt to not watch where I was going, but just concentrate on that spot. After several stumbles and falls, with continual practice you learn to expect the unexpected; it just becomes a habit. If you are continually watching your animals, you will have a pretty good idea as to how the herd's attitude will be.

8) Corral Designs

Corrals can be either hard or easy to work animals through. You don't need extra people standing around making a lot of unnecessary noise. It's loud enough just from the clanging and banging of the chute. I also recommend there be no alcohol around until after you finish working the animals. Remember, slower is faster. If you are running around like a chicken with his head chopped off, it is harder to get anything accomplished, much less get the bison to cooperate. Work the animals on their time, not yours. If you are in a hurry, or in a bad mood, the bison will sense it and make it that much harder to get things done.

A couple of good places to acquire corral designs are the Temple Grandin webpage and the Alberta Bison Association (ABA). The ABA has a book of very good people- and bison-friendly corral designs. Also, you can't beat a road trip to several bison ranches to view their corral systems, especially when they are working their bison through the corrals. My reasoning behind this is that you can get a feeling for what works and what doesn't.

9) Bison, Where It All Started

Bison have been residents of this rock we call Earth for some six hundred thousand years. They descended from an ancient species of cattle, Bos leptobos that lived on the forest's edge roughly one million years ago. Bison priscus was the first of several known species of bison. B. priscus appeared on the scene somewhere between six hundred thousand and three hundred thousand years ago, on the grassland steppes of Russia. B. priscus was one of today's bison's larger ancient relatives; in fact, today's modern bison are the smallest of the ancient bison's known relatives. B. priscus horns are noteworthy, as they curved forward and up and then swept back. B. priscus crossed over from Russia to North America via the Bering land bridge some three hundred fifty thousand to four hundred thousand years ago.

The next bison to make its presence felt was the giant of the bison world, Bison latifrons. B. latifrons stood a good 20 percent taller than today's bison, somewhere between seven to eight feet at the shoulder, or top of the hump. They are sometimes called the long-horned bison because their horns came straight out from the side of his skull. Total horn span was seven to eight feet from tip to tip.

Artifacts from B. latifrons have been discovered all over North America; it is one of the few species of bison whose remains have been discovered in what is now California.

Roughly twenty-five thousand years ago the pace of bison evolution picked up. Bison antiques replaced B. latifrons. B. antiques were smaller than its gigantic predecessor and had smaller horns. Both B. latifrons and B. antiques ranged from the west coast across the prairies toward the east coast. Bison occidentalist replaced B. antiques over 90 percent of its original range. B. occidentalist lived only about five thousand years and then today's bison replaced it roughly ten thousand years ago.

9.1) Today's Bison

Today there is a debate among members of the scientific community as to whether there are two or three subspecies of bison. There is also discussion as to whether bison should be classified as Bison or Bos/cattle for scientific reference. This I will leave to the scientists who do classification. I will list the subspecies from the smallest to the largest.

The European bison, or wisent (Bison bonasus), is the smaller of the three subspecies, and unlike his two relatives, he is more of a browser than a grazer. His neck muscles attach to his head differently, and he has adapted to surviving on leaves and tree bark, as he is mainly found in Poland's Bialowieza National Forest. These bison are an endangered species, with roughly one thousand living in both the wild and in zoological gardens throughout the world. B. bonasus has less hair than either of the other two species of bison but more on its tail, which is like a horse's tail. These bison look like a larger, stronger version of Africa's wildebeest.

Size-wise they are slightly smaller than their cousins. A mature wisent bull stands five to five and one half feet tall at the shoulder and averages one thousand to twelve hundred pounds in weight. The cows are lucky if they reach five feet at the shoulder and average seven hundred fifty to eight hundred pounds when mature.

The most numerous of the three species of bison are the plains bison (Bison bison). These are also the bison with the greatest amount of hair. Bulls, upon reaching full maturity at seven years of age, stand six feet tall at the top of the shoulder and weigh somewhere between eighteen hundred and twenty-three hundred pounds. Mature cows will stand somewhere between five to five and a half feet tall at the shoulder and tip the scales in a range from eight hundred to one thousand pounds every once in a while, you will find a really large cow that reaches twelve hundred pounds. These are the bison that are raised in our national and state parks, wildlife refuges, zoos and on private ranches today.

Our Canadian neighbors have North America's only pure herd of woods bison (Bison athabasca). These bison are taller, have less hair, especially on the front end, and have a slight dip or break along their topline.

All three of these bison interbreed quite easily, and none of their offspring are sterile. Scientists in both Canada and the United States have done genetic testing on both the plains and wood bison and have not been able to find any differences between the two species. Perhaps the wood bison could be a genetic hiccup having more to do with their environment than with their genes. We will delve into this issue in the chapter on genetics.

9.2) Migration: Did It Happen?

Gregarious, what does that word mean when pertaining to bison? According to Webster's Dictionary, gregarious means to be sociable, to join or form into groups. This applies directly to bison; they are highly sociable herd animals, and it also refers to the bison's choice of travel as they move from one place to another, across their range. There is no set time, reason, or season. They just up and go, it's in their blood, and they love to roam. And they will generally be in every part of their home range/pasture that's available to them, a complete circuit daily. My hypothesis for these seemingly errant wanderings has more to do with the need to find new forage, water, and minerals.

Bison roamed across the North American continent prior to the Big Kill, in a territory encompassing roughly eleven thousand miles. Skeletal remains have been found from just south of the Arctic Circle to the Northern provinces of Mexico, and from the Palouse country of Washington and Oregon eastward to almost the Atlantic Ocean. Approximately nine billion acres—this was the historic bison range.

There is and has been great speculation as to the number of bison and other wild ungulates this range could comfortably support. From my research on this subject, I have come across estimations ranging from a high of one hundred twenty-five million head to a low of thirty million head. Most accounts were between forty and sixty million head of bison. I favor Dr. Dale Lott's estimation of a herd size of thirty million animals and a state of dissemination/decline. In other words, they had already felt the pressure of indiscriminate hunting.

9.3) Behaviors: The Good, the Bad, and the Ugly—Know When to Walk Away; Know When to Run

Deciding to place this section on behaviors in this spot in the manuscript is important, as I have given you the basics on the natural history of the bison. The next section will awaken you to the signs that a bison will give you that you MUST be aware of while working with the bison or observing the bison, or while you are in the vicinity of these American icons. I am attempting to enlighten you, the public, as to how you can learn to read these signs and remain safe.

Bison display aggression through the use of body posture and tail position. Other combative postures one needs to be aware of are:

1. a determined advance; a stalking walk toward the intruder;

2. a swinging of the head from side to side, often accompanied by pawing and hooking of the earth; and

3. Last but not least, a series of bluff charges.

Tail position is also a quick, dependable way to read a bison's attitude should you accidentally come across one while traveling. Wes Olson has spent years learning about bison. In his book *Portraits of Bison*, he discusses several signals you should know:

- When a bison is in a state of rest and not disturbed, the tail will be hanging down, slightly away from the body.
- When the tail is out away from the body, level with the back with tassel hanging down, he has noted an item of interest. The bison's eyes will be focused upon the item of interest.

- A bison's next tail response to elevated aggression is to position the tail in an arch above the horizontal of the back; this is often noticed when new animals are introduced to the herd.
- When one notices a bison's tail standing up in a question mark and shaking rapidly, accompanied by the bison lowering his head and pawing and hooking the ground, it's time to exit stage right.

This tail position will hold true unless you inadvertently find yourself between a bison cow and her calf. She will just come at a high rate of acceleration, without a warning sign but with mayhem to the offender. Throughout my career I have noticed all of these signs and have developed a great respect for these animals and how much power they can send your way at any given moment.

Some other signs you need to be aware of while working bison through a corral system are: As they become more agitated, the vessels in the eyeballs will dilate to the point of bursting, and the eyeball itself will bulge, also in this list are licking, huddling, milling (a mass circular movement), backing up, and balking.

As fear levels escalate, one will notice bulging eyes; incoherent running, goring, or hooking of other bison; and trying to escape the confines of the corral by any means possible. The final state of elevated aggression would be toxic immobility. As this stage of aggression appears, the most marked sign you will see is the turning under of the ankle joints, and they will be moving around on these joints and not their hooves. The best thing you can do is isolate the animal, along with quiet, and no disturbance. These signs of elevated stress/agitation levels result in at least a 20 percent loss in weight for the animal, with each half hour that the producer keeps his animals in an escalating state of agitation, which in turn can result in loss of income to the producer, loss of body condition for the animals, and at the extreme end, either injury or death to the handlers or the animals.

For someone unaccustomed to these warning signs, bison are very unpredictable and dangerous. Those of us who are accustomed to dealing with bison on a day-to-day basis have a pretty good idea of what the bison are telling us, and it is reasonably safe to be around them. Remember that handlers must *always* be aware of what the bison are telling them and *always* leave themselves a way out.

Now that you are aware of some of what the bison are telling you, I'll try to inform you of what the bulls and cows are telling you. First, bison bulls don't want or need to waste energy fighting if they can accomplish the desired outcome without fighting for breeding rights. Rivals tend to try to accomplish this through posturing. If they cannot accomplish the desired outcome through posturing, then the impact will be felt throughout the surrounding countryside, along with their roaring. Fights are relatively short, usually not more than a couple of minutes, with the victor taking the prize. Bison give off enough signs as to what they are going to do; you just need to be observant enough to figure out what they are telling you.

If you happen to see your bison running along a fence with their heads up, they are measuring the height of the fence to see if they can possibly jump it. You only see this happening if they are being pursued by you or by another bigger, stronger, more dominant bison. I have seen a bison cow repeatedly crash a two-inch pipe corral until she obtained her freedom.

Speaking of running fences, it is always a good idea to keep a close eye on older cows or bulls for a while after bringing them into your herd. Older bulls, if they weren't raised on the place, generally have a hard time adjusting to new surroundings and will tend to want to go back whence they came—especially if they have a lot of competition for breeding rights from established herd bulls.

When you bring new animals into an established herd, there is going to be some serious pushing and shoving, as they need to find their place in the herd's pecking order or rank within the group.

A way to relieve some of this pushing and shoving is to have a pen or pasture right next door so they can get acquainted across the fence line.

9.4) Personal Encounters

In my dealings with bison, it hasn't all been fun and games. I should state here that when I first started making a partial living with bison I used to, and still do, work bison for other producers. I have learned a few lessons the hard way, taught to me by my furry friends, and these lessons took only one time to sink in.

I was once flung up against my back inside of a chute trying to get a yearling heifer to stand up in the chute. This was before I was aware of the Hot-Shot trick, and it resulted in a severe headache and my wearing a hard hat the next couple of times I worked bison.

Another incident took place at the Farm Show Grounds during the Eastern Bison Association Show and Sale. I was the yard foreman at this show and sale from its inception. As we were running animals up to the sale ring, we had a cow that just didn't want to enter the ring. The alleyways were a little over three feet wide, maybe closer to five feet in most spots. As our pens were built from corral panels borrowed from a local rodeo producer and set up on concrete floors, they tended to slide whenever an animal hit or bumped into them. They were built bison-tough, high, and strong. We were going smoothly until we got to the bison cow class. The first cow left her pen and went to the ring, no problem. The second got in the alleyway, ran up to the gate, turned around, and came all the way back. I happened to be on the outside of the ring, putting animals away as they exited the ring. I got called over to the inside of the ring, as they couldn't get the cow to take her turn in the spotlight, so to speak. She was heading for the ring gate, and I was at the gate, three-quarters of the alleyway down through the pens. I entered the alleyway and stepped up on the fence. As I was doing this, I told the crew members to get the black plastic to move her into the ring. Next thing I knew, my lower legs were smashed into the fence, and I was being lifted to the top rail of the fence. I extricated my right leg from her left horn and put it over the top rail. The crew got her into the ring with one try, and I went to the hospital. Turned out she just sliced the top layer of skin.

I wanted to add this to warn you never to think you know it all because something will turn up unexpectedly and bite you when you least expect it. Use caution; it is better than false bravado— you aren't bulletproof. Shows and sales are where the ugly behaviors make their presence felt, especially with mature cows.

Mature bison cows have no sense of humor; they don't like to be run around several times until the judge makes his decision, and the pens they are housed in at sale are usually ten feet by ten feet; small compared to their home pasture and very loud and noisy.

9.5) Words of Wisdom

I feel this would be a good place to add a few rules for working with and around bison:

• Do not be in a hurry; work your animals on their time, not yours. Slower is faster.

• Be aware of their ever-fluctuating flight and pressure zones. When in a corral situation, the handler is more than likely deep inside of this zone, so everything becomes more pronounced.

• Slow and steady movements are more effective than fast, jerky ones.

• No yelling, screaming, or waving of arms; these increase stress in bison.

• Do not try to block or stop an animal. Let it go past; she or he will return.

• Watch your animals at all times.

• Try to bucket train your animals with grain chop or range cake; get them used to eating it a couple of weeks prior to when you want to catch them. Don't feed them at all the day before you want to catch them. The next morning, feed in the corrals. I guarantee they will catch themselves.

All animals learn from experience. It is best to let your bison wander through the corral system several days before working them. They may find that the corral system is a reasonably safe place.

10) Genetics

Genetics in the bison industry today can be exciting and a very challenging topic of discussion among the producers, conservation groups, and national organizations. The reason for this is the crossbreeding experiments done by a few of the early saviors of the bison in the late 1800s. C. J. Buffalo Jones in Kansas, Charles Goodnight in Texas, and Canadian government entities were all trying to produce a hardy breed of cattle that could survive on the open range in winter. These first attempts at crossbreeding English breeds with bison were more or less forced breeding's, often ending with the death of the beef cow and calf due to a high amount of amniotic fluid, hydropsey, in the last trimester of the gestation period.

The above cross was the result of crossing a bison bull with an English cow. It seems that the idea of a better range animal took up a strong position in the minds of these early saviors of the bison. Because these early producers switched the cross around the opposite way, beef bull to a bison cow, the result was a viable live calf. Offspring from this F1 cross were viable females and sterile bulls, like a mule. In a pasture setting, it is highly unlikely that a breeding such as the above-mentioned breeding's would ever take place, as cattle and bison don't usually seek each other's company, except if there are only a couple of bison running with a cow herd on the same pasture and no bison bull present.

I found my genetics course in college to be very fascinating and very confusing at the same time. This was mostly due to the various terms used in the course. A few of the more confusing ones for me were:

Genotype: This is the specific set of traits or genetic constitution of an organism—the distinguishing characteristics that make a bison a bison. To say an animal is phenotypically a bison means that the traits you are looking at—what you see—make the animal a bison.

Heterozygous and homozygous: To explain the meanings of these terms, I'll use a past experience. Several years back, a ranch where I was herdsman had several different body types of mature plains bison bulls. There was one bull that bred true; he was a homozygous bull. All of the calves he sired looked exactly like young versions of their sire. It didn't matter which cows he bred, they all looked like their dad. On the other hand, several of the other bulls at this ranch would have a few calves that resembled their sire in build, stature, and attitude, but you could also see their mother's contribution in the mix. This would make those bulls that bred those cows' heterozygous or untrue breeders. They were still bison, but by looking at these animals phenotypically, you couldn't tell who their father was.

There are several exciting things happening in the field of bison genetics today. The first is better DNA tests. Dr. David Derr at Texas A&M leads the genetic field with his research on the bison genome.

The second is that the American Bison Society, along with the bison specialists group and the Wildlife Conservation Society, is funding a group of scientists to do genetic mapping of the bison genome, from its ancient relative's right through to today's bison. When the dust settles from all this genetic research, we, as producers and enthusiasts, should have a good idea where we are as far as diversity within the bison gene pool, what genes we have lost or gained over the course of time, how closely related our bison are to each other, and what effect cattle introgression has had on our bison of today's herds.

I feel that one of the biggest mistakes that we, as producers, are making today is our selection of animals based on genetic purity. Granted, probably a good percentage of the ranch-raised bison today have a very small percentage of cattle markers within their genetic makeup. That does not make them any the less bison, as these markers are passed down on the maternal side, but after generations upon generations of being bred back with bison, they are basically bison. Sure, the markers are there, but their influence is greatly limited. Any trace of cattle phenotype has long been erased. They are bison—not 100 percent bison but in the 95 to 99 percent range. If they act like bison and smell like bison, they are bison.

11) **Bison: Wild or Domesticated? That Is the Question**.

I am inserting this chapter on classification by both the federal and state governments, as it has become an issue in the state of Montana with the *wild* Yellowstone bison versus the ranch-raised *domestic* bison. I have some news for the protestors: I have been around both types of bison, and there is no difference. They are all just bison. Sure, the domestic bison are ranch raised and human influenced, but they are not, and will never be, domesticated.

They are treated like cattle, which they aren't. If anything, they are more liked a giant wild herd of sheep. Sure, the bison organizations have selectively bred these animals for certain traits such as heavier hindquarters, smaller humps, and faster rate of gain, and they have selectively culled the truly bad actors to take out some of the danger involved when working with these animals. Yet they are still bison; a little inbred perhaps, which pops up every once in a while, yet they remain bison.

Man, in his never-ending need to dominate everything and anything around him, still hasn't succeeded in ruining one of nature's great truly wild ungulates. In the last few years, some conservation groups that have bison herds under their influence have been actively culling out bison that have even a small percentage of cattle introgression/markers in their DNA, as they seem to feel that they are not raising a pure bison. As I stated earlier, all bison and cattle sprang from an ancient form of wild cattle. Who, and what, makes an animal a pure type of anything?

I feel that if we need to classify bison as wild or domestic, why not use the terms semi-restricted or restricted and leave it at that? This has to do with their lines of containment. The bison of Yellowstone have an imaginary park boundary line, and if they cross over it during the winter, they have to be back in the park by a certain day in May or suffer the consequences. These are man's rules, not the bison's. However, ranch-raised bison are restricted by fences and are usually pretty well-liked by their neighbors.

12) Hey, Doc, Am I Healthy or Not?

I feel that you can't do a book about bison management strategies without adding a chapter dealing with health issues in bison.

The first and most important issue, especially for producers raising bison in the east, central, and southern United States, is internal parasites. I recently had a client whose bison operation in southeast Illinois had a bout of both internal parasites and coccidiosis in his herd of twenty-nine bison. When he called me, he was fit to be tied; he had nine head left. He hadn't built a corral system yet. I knew what the problem was when he explained what the symptoms were. I told him to have his man gather some stool samples from various members of his herd and take them to his vet so we could determine the treatment. When the results came back, I told his man to go to the feed store and get some Safe-Guard worming blocks, which are basically a mixture of molasses and worming medicine that you place on the ground or feed bunk. I told him to get six blocks—that way he would have the next set of blocks for two weeks after he treated them the first time.

For treatment of coccidiosis, he needed to get corrid, which you mix with water. This treatment is repeated after twenty-one days. It is necessary to keep the animals in the same pasture until after you finish treating them a second time, and then move them. It is always a good idea to mow down the pasture and drag it, and then let it rest. This accomplishes two things. First, it busts up the manure clods; second, it causes the worm eggs, larvae, and adults exported in the dung to be exposed to the atmosphere, which should kill them. Letting the pasture rest is vital for the health of the grass and the soil.

These treatments are necessary anytime your ranch is in a climate that is moist and humid. Bison in this climate need to have this issue addressed at least twice a year, if not three or more times. Depending on the situation, the number of animals versus number of pastures, you as a producer must be aware at all time, the necessity of doing this for the animal's health. Another parasite, especially in the southern United States, is liver flukes, which are a little tricky finding if your animals have them. If you suspect your bison are wormy, take some stool samples to your vet. If the results come back within normal limits, wait a week and observe your bison for further loss of condition. Call your vet and have the tests done for flukes. The only treatment I am aware of for liver flukes would be Ivormec Plus. This is what I call a *catch-all wormer*, as it takes care of 99 percent of the internal and external parasites.

Hint:

DO NOT keep using the same wormer season after season or the worms will eventually build up a resistance to the medicine. Rotate the wormers that you use yearly; this will eliminate a buildup of resistance.

13) I wasn't aware there were so many bugs out in bison land

In this part of bison health, I will borrow from Dr. David Hunter's part of the Bison Breeders Handbook, published by the National Bison Association. I do this as I am not a veterinarian and I don't claim to know more about disease issues of bison than the professionals do.

Brucellosis/Bang's disease: This pathogen was first brought to this country by European settlers through the livestock they brought with them. We are still fighting brucellosis today. Every state has a regulation that all animals either passing through or landing within their borders be tested for brucellosis and TB within thirty days of shipment. It is also wise to check with the state veterinarian to find out what other tests their state may require for importation. Brucellosis will cause female ungulates to abort their offspring, meaning economic loss to the producer. Some states require that any bison/cattle females be calf hood vaccinated for brucellosis prior to being allowed into the state. This must be done when females are between six months and one year of age.

Bovine tuberculosis/TB: This is a slow, progressive bacterial disease. It can spread between species, including humans. In its early stages of development, it is difficult to diagnose. As the disease progresses, some of the symptoms are emaciation, weakness, and lethargy, which will result if left untreated in pneumonia with a chronic, moist cough. All states require that animals coming into their state be tested for TB.

This test is a three-day test. Animals are injected in the caudal fold of the tail and must be run through the handling facility three days later to have the tests read by the veterinarian, by means of palpation. If there is no change, the test is negative, meaning the animals are safe to transport.

Trichomonosis: This is what in today's society would be called an STD, or sexually transmitted disease. When you're purchasing new bulls, it is a wise idea to have them semen tested and have a test run for this disease. Most western states require a negative trich test on all bovine bulls for import and export. This disease can have massive economic consequences for any producers who have an outbreak within their breeding herd. Not only will their calf production be greatly affected, until the herd is treated and the suspect bulls removed, they won't be able to sell breeding bulls to anyone, anywhere.

I've only touched on a few of the main health issues that a producer needs to be aware of. Have a good working relationship with your vet, and do all you can to help him or her do the required tests. Most vets don't have a great deal of knowledge when it comes to working with and around bison. Don't expect them to help you gather your animals, and don't complain if it seems as if it takes too long for them to accomplish the job you hired them to do. It is part of your job to send them in the direction necessary or educate them to the fact that bison are not cattle. There are some big basic differences.

13.1) Medicating, the Healthful Advantage

All medications that you can give your animals are given either orally, by injection, or topically. Oral medications are given either in a bolus or pill with a balling gun or mixed in their drinking water. It helps if you can add a couple of packs of Kool-Aid along with the medication. Make sure that their only source of water is the tank that has the medication in it, and keep the animals locked in the corrals until the water and meds are all consumed.

Injected medications are given as a shot either under the skin (subcutaneously), in the heavy muscle of the neck (inter muscular), or by IV, which we seldom do with bison. All injections need to be given along the neck of the animal being treated.

Topically given medications are either pour-on or topdressing on food. Some of these medications are given by the weight of the animal, and if you don't have a chute and scale, you need to be a pretty good guesser of the weights on your animals. If you happen to give them too much, you could kill them—just a word of caution.

14) Marketing

There is a plethora of ways to market your bison.

You can **direct market your bison through several meat purveyors** who will buy your surplus bison at a price per pound per animal. If you are doing it this way, check the USDA marketing web page, click other under Species, and check the prices for whatever age your animals are for the price per pound data. This will give you a ballpark figure that you can expect for your animals.

You can **direct market them yourself**. Take them to the state or federal slaughter plant, pay the slaughter and inspection fees, and sell the meat yourself. I tried doing this once and was shut down in three days. This happened when I first got into the bison business. I forgot to check with the state I was living in as to the regulations pertaining to the sale of inspected bison meat. First, I didn't have a walk-in freezer or a certified scale. Chalk one up to the ignorance of how state governments work. I was naïve enough to think that if they could sell meat out of home freezer units in a neighboring state, I would be able to do it in the state I was living in at the time. Be sure to check all of your state rules and requirements pertaining to the sale of meat, what the requirements are, and the equipment needed to do so.

As I am sitting here typing this chapter, I am wishing that I were about four hours south of Bowman watching the Custer State Park annual bison roundup, which brings to mind the reason for this roundup. Each fall CSP does this so they can regulate the size of their bison herd in relation to the forage available to carry the herd through the winter. They usually run somewhere between three hundred and four hundred head through the sale ring at the park. This is the longest-running live public bison auction in the country, and they have helped start a lot of ranch herds through this sale. The CSP sale is typically the third weekend in November and is usually the first bison auction every year.

When I first ventured into the bison business, there weren't very many bison sales going on across the country. It was mainly Custer State Park, South Dakota, and the National Western Stock Show in Denver, Colorado. Since that time, the old National Buffalo and the American Buffalo Association have joined forces; in 1995, they merged to become the National Bison Association, which led to the formation of numerous state organizations. Several of these state organizations hold their own bison auctions at various localities across this nation. To find out where and when these live animal auctions take place in or near your area, contact the National Bison Association Office either via phone or on the web at www.bisoncentral.com.

You can conduct **private treaty sales**, in which you go to the producer, look at his whole herd, and look at the animals that he or she has for sale. Then you make your picks, call his vet and yours so you know what tests are required for entry into your state, schedule any testing, help with the testing of your animals, pay the person, load your animals, and take them home. It generally will take at least ten days for your animals to clear tests. After that, take your animal's home and enjoy.

15) The Native American View

I have several Native American friends I talk with once or twice a month. Some are experts in their fields of endeavor, mostly natural resources management, and others are just really good friends who are concerned about the plight of the Yellowstone bison (and bison in general).

Since I have been involved with and been around bison for a good part of my life, I have always been intrigued by the symmetry between the "Indian and the buffalo." I've asked questions but never really understood it until recently.

Native Americans use a three-point approach when it comes to bison. First, they consider bison to be relatives and a part of their religion. Bison were a mainstay and traveling commissary to the tribes. The second and third approaches are sort of intertwined, as usually their reservations contain a huge amount of undisturbed native prairie. The Native Americans see the bison as a healthy alternative—there is a high incidence of diabetes among the tribes, and the Native Americans believe restoration and conservation of bison placed on this earth is for the good of all of "the people" (as most tribes call themselves). I didn't fully understand what they were telling me until I read, over and over again, a couple of documents sent to me by Jason Baldes. Jason is a member of the Eastern Shoshone tribe in Wind River, Wyoming. He's studying to get his master's degree in restoration ecology from Montana State University in Bozeman, Montana. In his personal statement, Jason says: "Establishment of bison to the reservation will not only improve the ecological integrity of the area by restoration of a keystone species, but also contribute to the conservation of pure or genetically reputable bison while improving the culture and diet of tribal residents."

The Wind River Reservation is one of the first sites for location of surplus clean bison from Yellowstone Park in this ongoing restoration project. With all the hoops the Eastern Shoshone and Northern Arapaho tribes must go through to make it happen, people of Jason's caliber are the light at the end of the tunnel, which is drawing closer with each passing day.

I must add that one thing most Native Americans want is to let the bison be bison. Don't even try to make them into cattle, they are bison.

Through these writings, I have given you many things to consider, several ideas and facts. There are some subjects that I didn't include, as I am not aware of all facets of the given subject. For more information you can go to the sources listed in the bibliography or contact the National Bison Association or any of the local or state bison associations in your area. My hope is that you learned something from reading this book, and above all, I hope you enjoyed your trip about the business of raising bison.

Above all, keep your eyes open and have fun!

Works Cited by Chapter

Soil Health

Hillel, Daniel, *Out of the Earth: Civilization and the Life of the Soil*, University of California Press, 1991.

Holechek, Jerry L., Rex D. Pieper and Carlton H. Herbel, *Range Management: Principles and Practices*, 5th edition. Pearson Education, 2004.

Montgomery, David R., *Dirt: The Erosion of Civilizations*, University of California Press, 2007.

Gadzia, Kirk, *Holistic Management Workshop*, 2009, DVD.

Nature's Sun Collectors

Holechek, Jerry L., Rex D. Pieper, and Carlton H. Herbel, *Range Management: Principles and Practices*, 5th edition. Pearson Education, 2004.

Manning, Richard, *Grassland: The History, Biology, Politics and Promise of the American Prairie*. Penguin Books, 1997.

Seipel, T. and M. Lavin, *Common Plants of the North Central C. M. Russell Nation Wildlife Refuge and Adjacent American Prairie Reserve Lands*. World Wildlife Fund and Montana State University.

Savory, Alan and Jody Butterfield, _Holistic Management: A New Framework for Decision Making_. Island Press, 1999.

What's for Lunch?

Howell, Jim, and Alan Savory, _For the Love of Land: Global Case Studies of Grazing in Nature's Image_. Holistic Management International, 2008.

Savory, Alan, and Jody Butterfield, _Holistic Management: A New Framework for Decision Making_. Island Press, 1999.

Smith, Burt, _Moving 'Em: A Guide to Low Stress Animal Handling_. The Graziers HUI, 1998.

Vallentine, John, _Grazing Management_, 2nd edition. Academic Press, 2001.

Fencing, a Neighborly Necessity

This chapter was written from the school of hard knocks—all personal experiences, some learned the hard way, some not. There are numerous farm supply stores, county extension offices, and bison ranch producers that helped as I taught myself to build a bison-tight fence.

Corrals: You Got to Know When to Hold 'Em

My citations for this chapter are written from experience and observation, some lessons learned the hard way, except for the last part on corral design. I have listed those citations within the text. I have a good friend who has an extensive photo library of various handling facilities across this country. These facilities run the gamut from simple to grandiose; they are all working bison facilities. I try to glean the parts of a facility that grab my attention as being efficient and useful and incorporate them into a facility that I design.

Low-Stress Animal Handling, it works

For this chapter I used several websites:

www.budwilliams.com

www.managingwholes.com

www.templegrandin.com

www.handnhandlivestocksolutions.com

Smith, Burt, *Moving 'Em: A Guide to Low Stress Animal Handling.* The Graziers HUI, 1998.

Bison: Where It All Started

In this chapter on the natural history of bison I will cite the books I borrowed from for the whole chapter.

Lott, Dale F., *American Bison: A Natural History*, University of California Press, 2002.

Dary, David, *the Buffalo Book: The Full Saga of the American Animal*. Swallow Press/Ohio University Press, 1989.

McHugh, Tom, *the Time of the Buffalo*, Castle Books, 2004, First published 1972.

Mahoney, R. E., "Monarchs of Old," unpublished song, 1972.

Berger, J. and C. Cunningham, *Bison: Mating and Conservation in Small Populations*, Columbia University Press, 1994.

Geist, Valerius, *Buffalo Nation: History and Legend of the North American Bison*. Voyageur Press, 1996.
Brower, Jennifer, *Lost Tracks: Buffalo National Park 1909-1939*, Athabasca University Press, 2008.

Olson, W. and J. Janelle, *Portraits of the Bison,* University of Alberta Press, 2005.

Adams, S. M. and A. R. Dood, *Background Information on Issues of Concern for Montana: Plains Bison Ecology, Management and Conservation*, Montana Fish, Wildlife and Parks, 2011.

Behaviors: The Good, the Bad, and the Ugly—Know When to Walk Away; Know When to Run

A good portion of this chapter was from my own observations and experiences. Most of the signs of escalating stress in bison were garnered from various papers from the Temple Grandin website: www.templegrandin.com. Other information used includes:

Olson, W. and J. Janelle, *Portraits of Bison*, University of Alberta Press, 2005.

Mahoney, R.E., "Teaching Trust to Our Animals Is an Important Aspect of Handling," *The Buffalo Heard Magazine* (June and July 2003).

Hey Doc, Am I Healthy or Not?

This chapter was written from years of experience, roughly twenty, of dealing with this issue for various bison producers in and around the east coast.

I Didn't Know There Were So Many Bugs Out There in Bison Land

National Bison Association, *The Bison Producers' Handbook - A Complete Guide to Production and Marketing*. National Bison Association, 2010.

Marketing

Jennings, Dana C. and Judi Hebbring, *Buffalo Management and Marketing*, National Buffalo Association, 1983.

National Bison Association, *The Bison Producers' Handbook - A Complete Guide to Production and Marketing*. National Bison Association, 2010.

The Native American View

Zontek, Ken, *Buffalo Nation: American Indian Efforts to Restore the Bison.* University of Nebraska Press, 2007.

Other websites of interest are:

www.manageingwholes.com

www.stockmangrassfarmer.com

I left some headings out because 99 percent of the chapter was written from my own perspective on the subject of those chapters.

My hope is that you have learned something about our, hopefully, national mammal.

Made in the USA
Lexington, KY
17 February 2014